CONTENTS

Introduction

Cato's little distichs (or couplets) may be of little literary or philosophic importance in their own right,. But they have nonetheless had immeasurable influence in shaping the youth – and elders, and writers, and teachers- of countless generations, a school text in most countries of the then known worlds over centuries. As explained and illustrated in the accompanying essay, it stayed a best seller through centuries , effortlessly surviving the change from oral to manuscript to print, and is seemingly starting a revival today through the web.

This convenient edition is offered as an engaging text for learners of any age – how much more attractive than Caesar's marches through old-time France or made-up texts about sailors seeing the table (or, if you're lucky) the girl. It offers a truly accessible experience of *real* Latin as it was lived for centuries, and can serve at the same time as an introduction to the great literary corpus of Rome and its cultural heritage. Through the ages.

Perhaps with this handy edition of text and translation it can again become a school text? [6] [7]

CATO'S *DISTICHS*

the longest-running Latin primer

in a new edition, with commentary, by Ruth Finnegan

Callender Press 2013

ISBN 9781291546057

CATO DISTICHS

Latin text and English verse translation

Preamble

Telluris si forte uelis cognoscere cultus, Uergilium legito; quodsi mage nosse laboras Herbarum uires, Macer haec tibi carmina dicit; Si Romana cupis et Punica noscere bella, Lucanum quaeres, qui Martis praelia dixit; Si quid amare libet uel discere amare legendo, Nasonem petito; sin autem cura tibi haec est, Ut sapien uiuas, audi quae discere possis, Per quae semotum uitiis deducitur aeuum: Ergo ades et quae sit sapientia disce legendo.]

If it chances that thou desirest to learn farming, read Virgil. But if thou strivest rather to know the potency of herbs, Macer tells thee of this in his poems. If thou wishest to know about the Roman and Punic wars, enquire of Lucan who tells of the combats of Mars. If it takes thy fancy to love something or to learn by reading how to love, have recourse to Naso. But if thy chief desire is to live wisely, hear what thou canst learn about those things through which an old age free from vice is produced. So come and learn by reading what wisdom is. 8

Monostichs Deo *sntroductionupplica*. Parentes ama. Cognatos cole. Datum serua. Foro parce. Cum bonis ambula. Antequam uoceris, ne accesseris. Mundus esto. Saluta libenter. Maiori concede. Magistratum metue. Verecundiam serua. Rem tuam custodi. Diligentiam adhibe. Familiam cura. Mutuum da. Cui des, uideto. Conuiuare raro. Quod satis est, dormi. Coniugem ama. Iusiurandum serua. Uino tempera. Pugna pro patria. Nihil temere credideris. Meretricem fuge. Libros lege. Quae legeris, memento. Liberos erudi. Blandus esto. Irascere ob rem grauem. Neminem riseris. In iudicio adesto.

Pray to God. Love thy parents. Cherish those of kin to thee. Guard that entrusted to thee. Shun the market place. Walk with the upright. Attack not until you have challenged. Be neat. Salute freely. Yield to him who is older than thou. Respect the magistrate. Preserve thy sense of shame. Guard well thine own interests. Practice diligence. Care for thy family. Return like for like. Consider well to whom to make presents. Indulge rarely in banquets. Sleep enough. Love thy wife. Keep thy word. Be moderate with wine. Fight for thy country. Be not easily imposed upon. Shun the harlot. Read books. Remember what thou readest. See to the instruction of thy children. Be kind.

Cato's Distichs through the centuries

The longevity of quotations collections such as those of Thomas of Ireland from the eleventh century and Erasmus' long-running *Adages*, amazing as these are, was dwarfed by the remarkable diffusion and continuity of a short work known as Cato's *Distichs*, a book happily going on its way alongside these other productions. Little read now, this collection of Latin moralistic epigrams became one of the best-known books in the Middle Ages and earlier, and remained in circulation for well over a millennium. For much of that time it was a best-seller in both manuscript and print[1]

It apparently originated in late antiquity, possibly the third century AD, when the name of Cato became attached to the collection. It was a series of short pieces of moral advice in Latin verse. These were not attributed to earlier writers but presented as precepts by Cato himself, or at any rate credited to him. Some probably went back to Greek originals and many carried reminiscences of Latin poets such as Horace, Ovid, or Virgil, and at least one (2.3) was well-enough known to be quoted on an early gravestone:

Cease death to fear
none but a fool would choose
thro' fear of death the joys of life to lose.

'Cato's' collection came to be circulated as a store of memorable sayings in the same way as other compilations of quotation, had a huge circulation in many languages, and was extensively mined in later compilations of proverbs and moral maxims.

The book opened with a short prologue. As so often in the tradition of wisdom literature, the precepts were notionally addressed to the author's son:

When I noticed how very many go seriously wrong in their manner of living I concluded that I must apply a corrective to their belief and take counsel of the experience of mankind in order that they may live most gloriously and attain honour. Now I will teach thee, dearest son, in what way thou mayest fashion a rule for thy life. Therefore, so read my precepts that thou mayest understand them, for to read and not to understand is equivalent to not reading (Cato *Distichs*, Prologue, transl. Chase 1922).

Fifty-seven short one-line proverbial maxims followed, with pieces of practical and ethical advice like 'Yield to him who is older', 'Guard well your own interests', 'Keep your temper', 'Don't drink too much', 'Remember a good turn'.

The meat of the collection came in the following four books of (in all) 144 precepts in two-line classical Latin verse: the 'distichs' (couplets) of the title,1 the Latin of antiquity reproduced here and still read by modern students and their teachers..

Slim as it was, the collection had a long life before it. It did not spring directly from the Christian tradition so, unlike Thomas of Ireland's huge compilation or Erasmus' learned collection, could not carry the authority of excerpts from revered writers. Nor did it have an alphabetical ordering or other device for easy searching. Yet it was a best seller for centuries, adopted and adapted by the Christian church and distributed across diverse countries and languages.

The central reason for this continuing popularity was its use in education. It served both as a key text for the learning of Latin and as a source of moral wisdom – albeit of a fairly practical and worldly kind - for instructing the young. It was read in Roman primary schools in later antiquity, studied in seventh-century monastery schools in Ireland, and in both the British Isles and the Continent was on school textbook lists in the eighth to eleventh-centuries. It was often bound together with other selected works in standard (if changing) combinations for school use, and from the fifteenth century taken up by printing presses across the western world.

Prized both as moral guide and Latin primer it helped to shape many lives over the centuries. More than just a schoolbook, it was read and valued by adults too, quoted both by scholars and in popular songs, and the couplets, often learned by heart during schooldays, left their trace through later years. Its verse style influenced later gnomic collections, and for centuries it was alluded to by writer after writer as a taken-for-granted text. It was referred to by the French poet Venantius Fortunatus in the sixth century and used by a long series of famous authors over the centuries, from Alcuin and Gerald of St Gall to the English Alfred the Great who, it was said, drew on it for his proverb collection. From the twelfth century on, as one author puts it, 'references to Cato ... are to be found literally everywhere' (Hazleton 1957: 159). The fourteenth-century *Piers Plowman* quoted plentifully from the *Distichs*, acknowledging the source. Chaucer was closely acquainted with the collection. His *Canterbury Tales* had many quotations – and parodies - from 'Catoun which that was so wys a man', and he could rely on his audience's understanding when he characterised a carpenter as without the most elementary of learning since 'He knew no Catoun, for his wit was rude'. Cato was mentioned in the prologue to *Don Quixote,* and both mediaeval and later German and Spanish writers quoted him extensively. By the fifteenth and sixteenth century parodies were circulating in the vernacular, as in the *Schoole of Slovenrie: or Cato Turn'd Wrong Side Outward* (1605). Its popularity was both demonstrated and enhanced by numerous commentaries and expositions in both mediaeval and more recent times, themselves built on for further exposition and circulation.

CATONIS
DISTICHA MORALIA
EX CASTIGATIONE D.
ERASMI ROTERODAMI
una cum annotationibꝰ & ſcholijs
Richardi Tauerneri anglico
idiomate conſcriptis in
uſum Anglicæ iu-
uentutis.

LONDINI.
Ex ædibus Richardi Tauerner.
Anno. M.D.XL.

Cum priuilegio ad imprimen-
dum ſolum.

Title page of Richard Taverner's edition

Its massive diffusion also took place through innumerable translations – into, among other languages, French, German, Spanish, Danish, Dutch, Swedish, Italian, Polish, Hungarian, Irish, Anglo-Saxon, Anglo-Norman, Bohemian, Greek and Icelandic.

Four English editions of a version translated from the French were printed by William Caxton within seven years, the first in 1477; he dedicated it 'vnto the noble auncyent and renommed cyte [city] of London in Englond', directing it to the children of London merchants, as 'the best book to be taught to young children in school, and also to the people of every age it is full convenient if it be well understanded'. Erasmus quoted the book and brought out a version, itself widely translated and distributed in multiple editions, often bound together with other collections of wise sayings (Fig. 5.6 shows the title page of a London edition published in 1540). Another version, edited by Calvin's teacher Maturinus Corderius, was said to have gone through a hundred printings.

Sedechias was the first Philosophre by whom
through the wil and pleaser of oure lorde god
Sapience was vnderstande and lawes receyued. Whiche Sedechias saide that euery creature of good beleue ought to haue in hym sixtene vertues ¶ The first vertue is to drede and knowe god and his angellys ¶ The seconde vertue is to haue discrecion to discerne the goode from the badde and to vse vertu and flee vices ¶ The thride vertue is to obeye the kynges or princes that god hath ordeygned to regne vpon hym and that haue lordship and power vpon the people ¶ The fourthe vertue is to worship hys fadre & hys modre ¶ The fyfthe vertue is to do Justely and truely to euery creature aftir his possibilite ¶ The sixthe vertue is to distribute his almes to the pouer people ¶ The seuenthe vertue is to kepe and defende straungers and pilgrymes ¶ The eyghte

The first page of Caxton's print edition

In one form or another the book long continued in circulation. The Latin text was printed in 1577 as part of the Jesuits' educational programme in Mexico. It was used in English classrooms in the time of Milton and Oliver Cromwell, prescribed by sixteenth and seventeenth century statute for public schools like Eton and Harrow, and published with Erasmus' commentary in London in 1760 as *Cato's Distichs de moribus improved, in a more complete and useful method than any yet extant ... For the use of schools*. In both continental Europe and America its use in schools continued well into the eighteenth century in both Latin and vernacular. In 1735 Benjamin Franklin published a newly translated version in Philadelphia as *Cato's Moral Distichs Englished in Couplets* – the first Latin classic to be translated and printed in the British colonies of North America. He saw it as of good moral use for both adults and children – 'Very proper to be Put in the Hands of Young Persons' – and was confident that it would be in demand.

The Manuscript copy of this Translation of *Cato's Moral Distichs* happened into my Hands some time since, and being my self extremely pleased with it, I thought it might be no less acceptable to the Publick. ...In my Opinion it is no unfit or unprofitable Entertainment for those of riper Years. For certainly, such excellent Precepts of Morality, contain'd in such short and easily-remember'd

Sentences, may to Youth particularly be very serviceable in the Conduct of Life, since there can scarce happen any Affair of Importance to us, in which we may need Advice, but one or more of these Distichcs suited to the Occasion, will seasonably occur to the Memory, if the Book has been read and studied with a proper Care and Attention. ...

I confess, I have so great Confidence in the common Virtue and Good Sense of the People of this and the neighbouring Provinces, that I expect to sell a very good Impression (Franklin 1735: iii-iv).

Though Cato's text is no longer in print and is by now largely forgotten, it is gaining new life through circulation on the web and occasional surfacing in college courses. It even provided the 'quote for the day' (17th June) on a 2009 website, in its translation as:

Dread not the day that endeth all life's ills;
For fear of death all joy in living kills.
(helian.net/blog/2009/06/17/quote-for-today/quote-for-the-day-dionysius-cato-in-distichs/ 26 Nov. 2009).

These and other collections were constructed by their compilers from many, and varied, sources. The verbal clusters selected for record could be shorter or longer (sometimes just a single phrase or line); by unknown or by named (or misnamed) authors; and in a variety of familiar or unfamiliar languages. Depending on date or context they could be drawn from everyday or rhetorical speech, or – more often – from written sources: religious, literary, philosophical and much else, and presented under a variety of terms. Common at all periods, it seems, was some version of 'sayings' (Latin *dicta*) but with changing targets and connotations over the centuries. The 'authorities' of early collections, whether Christian or from the ancient classical world, gradually gave way or were combined with less normative terms like 'maxims', 'commonplaces' (with its changing meanings), 'proverbs', 'adages', the overarching term 'quotations' or, most recently, 'catchphrases', 'songs' and 'slogans'.

The selections were also of course bound into that same question as in the previous chapter: of whose voices and what kind of excerpts counted as suitable for highlighting, repeating and – in the present context – storing for further reference. Attitudes to the collecting of others' words have in part paralleled the changing uses of quote marks, as they gradually moved from focusing primarily on classical, literary or authoritative Christian sources to sayings from the near-present, from the 'common man, and from spoken not just written language. By the nineteenth century newspapers as well as literary and biblical sources were being drawn on and, though the idea of 'best authors' still prevailed, nineteenth- and, especially, twentieth-century quotation collections laid particular stress on 'familiar', 'popular', or 'in most frequent' or 'common' use. Not that that avoided the issue of *whose* definition of 'familiar' counted and who controlled the selection. In the sixteenth century Erasmus had presented his adages as 'frequently on people's lips' while looking to the ancient classic writers for his selection and despising the verbalisation of the common people, while the 'literary reader' of the 1941 *Oxford Dictionary of Quotations* might scarcely fit the common expectations of today. But the trawl has now certainly spread to include wording from film, broadcast and 'non-traditional' media, extending beyond the traditional literary canon of just one country. Recent collections boast of being up to the minute and pride themselves on including 'new', 'modern' and 'topical' quotes.

But at same time another striking feature of recent collections – even now - is a continuing interest in spanning the ages. Contemporary blurbs swim with phrases like 'from Cleopatra to J. K. Rowling, and the battle of Marathon to the Hutton inquiry', 'from the ancients of East and West to the global village of the twenty-first century', 'from Cicero to the Simpsons'. The sources come from past as well as present and, as in earlier collections, there remains a focus on the wealth and wisdom of past times. Even now allusions to the classical world carry surprising resonance and many collections still contain quotations from Latin or Greek and the high-art literary canon from earlier centuries, and refer in their blurbs to the authors of antiquity. Looking to the past not just the present almost seems a requirement for what it is to be a collection of quotations.

This is reinforced by the remarkable longevity of many key collections and their impact both across vast geographical areas and on successive generations. In their presence and travels they transmit, and embody, voices from beyond the present.

The Dictes and Sayings of the Philosophers published by William Caxton in 1477 is an example of one such compilations. That it should be the first book to be printed with a date in England evidences the interest in such collections while its curious history illustrates well both their long-lived potential and the complex and far-reaching pathways they sometimes followed. The Arabic original of this work had been compiled in Cairo near the start of the second millennium by the Syrian Mubashshir ibn Fatik as *Muhtar-al-Hikam* ('Wise sayings'). It appeared in 1053 with its hundreds of quotations from Jewish, Arabic and Greek sources. Two centuries later it was circulating in Spanish translation as *Bocados de Oro* ('Gold sayings'). It was soon translated further into Latin, cut down to just the philosophers' sayings, and circulated widely in Europe under such titles as *Liber philosophorum moralium* or *Placita philosophorum.* In the late fourteenth century it appeared in French as *Les dits des philosophes*. Both Latin and French versions became popular in England and at least four English translations were in circulation in the mid to late fifteenth century, with many changes and errors accumulated over the centuries. Caxton's 1477 publication was a translation from the French version into English by the king's brother-in-law Earl Rivers who paid Caxton to print and edit it (on this (arguably controversial) work see Raybould 2006, Jayne 1995: 37ff).)

Except in its remarkable long life, extended here, Cato's *Distichs* were far from unparallelled, a notable feature of the long-standing, and surely still valued, culture of Europe, and beyond Europe now offered once more to contemporary readers.

A collection of such longevity surely tells us something about the European devotion to written repositories of verbal sayings. Over the centuries there have indeed been many great literary works and collections but there can have been few which directly touched so many lives over a millennium or more as this modest compilation of maxims. A long tradition unquestionably underpins the quotation collections of today.

Note: I have drawn especially on Chase 1922 and Duff and Duff 1935, also on Boas 1952, Hazelton 1957, 1960, Marchand 2006/2009, Taylor 1992, 1999, 2004; see also references below. The traditional attribution to the earlier Roman statesman Marcius Portius Cato and the added name of Dionysius are rejected by modern scholars.

References

Boas, Marcus (ed.) (1952) *Disticha Catonis*, Amsterdam: North-Holland Publishing.

Chase, Wayland Johnson (1922) *The Distichs of Cato. A Famous Medieval Textbook*, Madison: University of Wisconsin Studies in the Social Sciences and History 7.

Duff, John Wight and Duff, Arnold Mackay (eds) (1935) *Minor Latin Poets*, London: Heinemann.

Finnegan, Ruth (2011) *Why Do We Quote? The Culture and History of Quotation,* Cambridge: Open Book, chapter 5 (also www.openbookpublishers.com/product.php/75/18/-why-do-we-quote--the-culture-and-history-of-quotation/)

Hazelton, Richard (1957) 'The Christianization of "Cato": the *Disticha Catonis* in the light of late mediaeval commentaries', *Mediaeval Studies* 19: 164-7.

Marchand, James and Irvine, Martin (eds and transl.) (2006/2009) *Cato's Distichs* http://ccat.sas.upenn.edu/jod/texts/monostich.html (July 2006), possibly replaced by www9.georgetown.edu/faculty/jod/texts/cato.html (15 Nov. 2009).

Taylor, Barry (1999) 'Michael Verinus and the *Distichs* of Cato in Spain: a comparative study in reception', in Taylor, Barry and Coroleu, Alejandro (eds) *Latin and Vernacular in Renaissance Spain*, Manchester: Manchester Spanish and Portuguese Studies.

Taylor, Barry (ed. and transl.) (2004) *Alonso de Cartagena(?) Cathoniana Confectio*, Bristol: HiPLAM.

Here foloweth The lyf of Saynt Iherome And first of his name

Iherome is sayd of Gerar that is holy / And of nemus / that is to saye a woode / And soo Gerome

PHIL

Printed and Sold by

ſion, will ſeaſonably occur to the Memory, if the Book has been read and ſtudied with a proper Care and Attention.

When I obtained Leave to make this Publication, I procured alſo the following Account of the Author and his Work: for I thought ſomething of the kind neceſſary to be prefix'd to it.

In moſt Places that I am acquainted with, ſo great is the preſent Corruption of Manners, that a Printer ſhall find much more Profit in ſuch Things as flatter and encourage Vice, than in ſuch as tend to promote its contrary. It would be thought a Piece of Hypocriſy and phariſaical Oſtentation in me, if I ſhould ſay, that I print theſe Diſtichs *more with a View to the Good of others than my own private Advantage: And indeed I cannot ſay it; for I confeſs, I have ſo great Confidence in the common Virtue and Good Senſe of the People of this and the neighbouring Provinces, that I expect to ſell a very good Impreſſion.*

Some

The PRINTER to the READER.

THE *Manuſcript Copy of this Tranſlation of* Cato's Moral Diſtichs, *happened into my Hands ſome Time ſince, and being my ſelf extreamly pleaſed with it, I thought it might be no leſs acceptable to the Publick; and therefore determined to print it as ſoon as I ſhould have convenient Leiſure and Opportunity. It was done by a Gentleman amongſt us (whoſe Name or Character I am ſtrictly forbid to mention, tho' it might give ſome Advantage to my Edition) for the Uſe of his own Children; But in my Opinion, it is no unfit or unprofitable Entertainment for thoſe of riper Years. For certainly, ſuch excellent Precepts of Morality, contain'd in ſuch ſhort and eaſily-remember'd Sentences, may to Youth particularly be very ſerviceable in the Conduct of Life, ſince there can ſcarce happen any Affair of Importance to us, in which we may need Advice, but one or more of theſe Diſtichs ſuited to the* Occa-

Some ACCOUNT of the following Piece, and Conjectures concerning its AUTHOR.

THO' the Original of these Moral Distichs, by being put into the Hands of Boys of the lower Forms at the Latin School, have been frequently considered as an Entertainment suitable only to such childish Years; yet great and able Judges have conceived a much more honourable Esteem of them. They have been commented on by divers Authors, but particularly by *Erasmus*: They were translated into Greek by *Maximus Planudes*, a native of *Greece*, and one of the most learned of his Age. But the great *Joseph Scaliger*, dissatisfyed with that Performance, gave another most elegant Version of them into the same Language, which has been divers times printed. And tho' a Critic in that Tongue, on viewing the Version, would not easily be induced to believe it could be better'd, yet it has been twice since attempted by two other several Hands, mentioned by *Fabricius*. So that at least four Greek Translations of them have appeared. Into the European Languages, as French, Italian, Dutch, there have been many Translations, and into each of them by several Hands. They have also been divers Times render'd into our own; but the Author of this never saw any of them, that by *Charles Hoole*, made in plain and low Language for the Use of School-boys, only excepted; and therefore he knows not but they may have been much better done before: But as he intended them (as they are here finished) solely for the Use of his own Children, with some of their Acquaintance, and never for publick View, he is no way solicitous what others may have perform'd, provided these as they are, will answer the End they were intended for. Those who find Fault with them may try to do better on any Score of them together, and then they will be more capable of judging, whether it is a very easy Task throughout the

B whole

CATO's

MORAL DISTICHS.

1.

IF God be Spirit, as old Texts assure,
Him chief o'er all with purest mind adore.

2.

Be still industrious, too much Sleep refrain;
For Vice from Sloth does constant Succours gain.

3.

Think the first Virtue's well to rule the Tongue;
He's godlike wise, who ne'er employs it wrong.

4.

Consistent always with thy self be found;
Who thwarts himself, would thwart all Mankind round.

5.

If o'er Mens Lives and Deeds thou cast an Eye,
While all spy Faults, free from them none thou'lt spy.

The

6.

The Charms of hurtful Joys, tho' ſweet, refuſe:
'Tis ſometimes Gain ev'n Wealth itſelf to loſe.

7.

Or grave or gay appear, to ſuit the Time:
The Wiſe may Manners change without a Crime.

8.

Let not your Wiſe's weak Humours Anger move
Againſt a Servant you've juſt Cauſe to love.

9.

When thou reproves a Friend, tho' ſcarce he'll bear,
Tho' much he frown, continue ſtill thy Care.

10.

Wage not with Men of Words, a noiſy War;
Words *all* have got, *Few* Wiſdom to their Share.

11.

So love thy Friends, and ſo thy Favours deal,
As that thy ſelf their Want may never feel.

12.

Spread not Reports, leſt they be thought thy own:
From Tatling Miſchief ſprings, from Silence none.

13.

Let not *another's* Promiſe *thine* engage
To plight thy Faith; 'tis now a faithleſs Age.

14.

When others praiſe thee, judge thy ſelf alone;
Better thou'rt to thy ſelf than others known.

15.

A Friend's good Offices aloud proclaim;
But thy good Deeds to others never name.

While

16.

While in Old-age you others Conduct tell,
Think whether in your Youth your own was well.

17

What Men in private whiſper, never mind;
The Guilty always think themſelves deſign'd.

18.

While Fortune's ſmiling, bear a watchful Eye
On her Reverſe, her Favours ſwiftly fly.

19.

Since on ſo frail a Tenure Life is held,
Thy Hopes on Death's Reverſions never build.

20.

The poor Man's Preſent from his ſcanty Store
With Thanks receive, as if its Worth were more.

21.

Since Nature form'd thee naked in the Womb,
Grudge not at Want; it does thy State become.

22.

Fear not the End of Life, it ends thy Care;
He preſent Life deſtroys, who Death does fear.

23.

When to thy Merit, Friends ungrateful prove,
Accuſe not Heaven, but with more Judgment love.

24.

Spare but to ſpend, and Spending ſpare ſo well,
As neither *now* nor *after* want to feel.

25.

Promiſe not twice what may at once be done,
Leſt thou be bounteous deem'd in *Words* alone.

26.

Him, who is kind in *Words*, but false in *Heart*,
In his own Coin repay, with Art for Art.
[*Yet with unblemish'd Honour act thy Part.*]

27.

No Stress on smooth-tongu'd Mens Professions lay;
Sweet plays the Fowler's Pipe to gain his Prey.

28.

If thou hast Children, but no Wealth to give,
Then teach them Arts, that they may learn to live.

29.

Mean things as Great, great things as *Mean* esteem;
So neither *prodigal* nor *near* thou'lt seem.

30.

Act not thy self what thou art wont to blame;
When Teachers slip themselves, 'tis double Shame.

31.

Crave what is Just and Honest, nought beside;
'Tis vain to ask what may be well deny'd.

32.

Th' unknown to what thou knows do not prefer;
For Judgment governs *here*, Chance only *there*.

33.

Since Life's frail Course through certain Danger lies,
Each new-come Day as a new Purchase prize.

34.

Tho' in the right, yield sometimes to a Friend;
Friendship by kind Complaisance is maintain'd.

35.

In quest of greater Matters, spare not small;
'Tis Profit that in Love unites us all.

With

36.

With Intimates no trifling Quarrels move;
Wrath *Hate* begets, Concord increases Love.

37.

When Servants Failings thy Resentments warm,
Thy Anger check, lest thou their Persons harm.

38.

Your Friends o'ercome not always when you can;
For Patience often speaks the greater Man.

39.

What thou hast gain'd with Toil, preserve with Care:
Heavy's the Task past Losses to repair.

40.

In Plenty let thy Friends thy Bounty share;
Yet make they self thy most peculiar Care.

BOOK II.

YOU who in Husbandry would Skill attain,
May *Virgil* read; or if you'd Knowledge gain
In healing Plants, these you'll in *Macer* find,
With Cures prescrib'd for Ails of every kind.
If Civil Wars and *Rome*'s sad Broils you'd know,
Lucan those dire Exploits of *Mars* will show.
Or if by Rules you'd guide Love's gentler Flame,
Ovid consult: But if your nobler Aim
To steer your Life by Wisdom's Laws aspire,
Read here, and learn the Prudence you desire.

1.

Even to Strangers thy good Deeds extend;
'Tis better than a Crown to gain a Friend.

2.

Search not God's Secrets, nor his Works on high;
Mind what concerns thee as thou'rt born to die.

3.

Avoid the Fear of *Death*, it idle ſhews
For fear of loſing *Life*, its *Joys* to loſe.

4.

Of Doubts contend not in an angry mind:
Wrath clouds the Soul, and does the Judgment blind.

5.

Genteely ſpend as Circumſtances crave:
'Tis ſometimes *Loſs* penuriouſly to *ſave*.

6.

Avoid Exceſs, purſue the Golden Mean;
'Tis ſafeſt Sailing in the gentle Stream.

7.

What gives thee Shame, reveal not unto more,
Leſt *Many* blame what but *One* blam'd before.

8.

Think not th'Unrighteous in their Crimes ſucceed;
Time that conceals reveals an impious Deed.

9.

No feebler Creature's Want of Strength deſpiſe;
For Nature Want of Strength by Skill ſupplies.

10.

When over-match'd, in time reſolve to yield;
Thus oft the Victor's by the Vanquiſh'd foil'd.

Shun

11.

Shun with thy Friends contentious Words to use;
For Discord oft from trifling Words ensues.

12.

All Search of Fate by Divination fly:
God without thee thy Lot decrees on high.

13.

Create not Envy by a sumptuous Dress;
For tho' it hurts not, 't may affect thy Peace.

14.

Be not dismay'd when Judges do thee Wrong;
The Cause that's gain'd unjustly, thrives not long.

15.

In Quarrels past name not what was unkind:
To think on't argues an ungenerous Mind.

16.

Nor praise nor blame thy self, for only Fools
Thus court Vain-glory by preposterous Rules.

17.

Manage with Care thy Wealth, Expence restrain;
Th' Estate's soon lost that took long time to gain.

18.

A Fool, when there's Occasion for't, appear;
'Tis sometimes *Wisdom*, *Folly*'s Mask to wear.

19.

With equal care avoid a Miser's Name
And *Prodigal*'s; they both will wound thy Fame.

20.

Believe not all, some kind of People tell;
They talk not always true, who talk a deal.

21.

Forgive not what thou dost provok'd by Wine;
'Tis not the Liquor's fault; to drink was *Thine*.

22.

Thy Counsels to a trusty Friend declare;
Thy Health commit to wise Physicians Care.

23.

At worthless Mens Advancement never grieve:
Who highest mount, the heaviest Fall receive.

24.

Still for the Worst to come, thy Mind prepare;
So with more Ease thou Ills foreseen wilt bear.

25.

In adverse Times let not thy Courage fail:
Still hope, 'gainst Hope ev'n Death can scarce prevail.

26.

Slip not the Season when it suits thy Mind;
Time wears his Lock *before*, is bald *behind*.

27.

View well what's past, and what may next ensue,
And Janus-like at once both Seasons view.

28.

Thy Health to guard, Pleasures sometimes refrain;
To Pleasure somewhat give, but Health's the Main.

29.

Slight not the general Vogue while thou'rt but one,
Lest while thou slights the most thou pleases none.

30.

Manage thy Health 'bove all with prudent Care,
Nor for thy Follies blame th' unwholesome Air.

Regard

31.
Regard not Dreams, the Mind will ſtill purſue
In *Sleep*, what *waking* it had moſt in View.

BOOK III.

WHOE'ER will on theſe Lines ſome Thoughts beſtow,
Which wholeſome Rules for Life's ſure Conduct ſhow,
Will reap th' Advantage: Thoſe who them deſpiſe
Will prove not *mine*, but *their own* Enemies.

1.
No Pains t' adorn thy Mind with Knowledge ſpare;
Without it Life does Death's dull Image bear.

2.
For Loſs of Pelf 'gainſt Fortune don't exclaim;
Virtue not Wealth gives Happineſs and Fame.

3.
Scandal, while thou uprightly acts, deride:
'Tis not in human Power Mens Tongues to guide.

4.
When as an Evidence thou muſt appear,
Favour thy Friend, but keep thy Conſcience clear.

5.
Againſt ſoft ſoothing Speeches guard thy Heart;
Truth Plainneſs chooſes, *Fraud* diſſembling Art.

6.
To Sloth, Life's great Conſumption, give not way;
Sloth in the *Mind* does on the Body prey.

By

17.

When Laws oppreſs, Aid from the Judge deſire;
For Laws ſome Mitigation oft require.

18.

What thou from Juſtice ſuffers, calmly bear,
And on thy Guilt thy ſelf be moſt ſevere.

19.

Read much, and much of that when read reject;
For Poets Wonders more than Truth affect.

20.

At Feaſts in Talk be modeſt, leſt thou gain
A Trifler's Name while ſtudying t' entertain.

21.

Regard not Woman's Paſſions, nor her Smiles:
With *Paſſion* ſhe enſnares, with *Tears* beguiles.

22.

Enjoy thy Goods, but let no Waſte be made:
Who waſtes his own, will others Right invade.

23.

Firmly reſolv'd, Death's Summons ſcorn to fear,
Which if not lovely, ends at leaſt all Care.

24.

If thy Wife's virtuous, bear her Tongue, for ſure
Thou may'ſt for her good Deeds ſome Words endure.

25.

Equal Affection for both Parents bear;
Nor ſlight the one the other to revere.

BOOK IV.

YOU who a Life secure from Ills would lead,
And Virtue's Paths by Vice untainted tread,
Firmly impress these Precepts on your Mind,
Here by your self you'll safe Direction find.

1.

Riches contemn if thou true Bliss would find;
Who honour these, are Beggars in their Mind.

2.

If by wise Nature's Rules thou bounds Desires,
Thou'lt easy live; 'tis little she requires.

3.

For Ills that from thy own Imprudence came,
Thy own weak Folly not thy Fortune blame.

4.

The Use of Money not the Metal prize;
Souls truly great will ever that despise.

5.

To keep thy Body sound, spare not thy Wealth:
Riches are tasteless when not blest with Health.

6.

If when at School the Master's Rod thou bore,
Bear with a Parent's Anger much the more.

7.

In Things of real Use thy Time employ;
Vain Projects Time and Money both destroy.

8.

Sell not thy Favours through unkind Delays,
But Friends, the nobleſt Purchaſe, with them raiſe.

9.

When thou ſuſpects a Miſchief, ſtrait enquire;
Neglected Sparks oft raiſe deſtructive Fire.

10.

When *Venus* through thy Blood enflames Deſire,
Retrench thy Food; high Feeding fans the Fire.

11.

Devouring Beaſts Man juſtly dreads, yet know
That Man to Man is the moſt *dreadful Foe.*

12.

If thou excells in Strength, direct it well;
So may thou in true Valour too excel.

13.

In Straits a well-prov'd Friend's Aſſiſtance crave:
In Straits no Doctor like a Friend can ſave.

14.

Why for thy Guilt ſhould guiltleſs Victims bleed;
By others Death thou cann't from Death be freed.

15.

When ſome true Boſom-Friend thou ſeeks to chooſe,
Let Wiſdom and not Wealth direct thy Views.

16.

Vile Avarice deteſt, enjoy thy Store:
The Miſer midſt his Heaps of Wealth is poor.

17.

If thou a Fame unblemiſh'd would'ſt maintain,
Th' alluring Charms of Vice with Care refrain.

In

18.

In Youth mock not old Age; Youth swiftly spends,
And double Childhood human Life attends.

19.

Still learn some useful Thing, for small's the Cost,
Yet that may hold when all Things else are lost.

20.

In Silence ponder well what others say:
Words oft the Speaker's inward Soul betray.

21.

When thou hast gain'd a Science, practice still;
Practice in every Art improves the Skill.

22.

With future Ills thy Soul ne'er terrify:
Who Life despises needs not fear to die.

23.

Learn of the Learn'd, and others teach again,
That useful Knowledge thro' the World may reign.

24.

Drink not beyond thy Strength; for from Excess
Disorders spring that the whole Frame distress.

25.

What you've approv'd in publick, don't again
Condemn through Lightness; 'twill your Credit stain.

26.

In *prosperous* Times don't on their Stay presume:
In *adverse*, hope for better still to come,

27.

Cease not to learn, Wisdom's by Care attain'd,
And Prudence from a long Experience gain'd.

Sparingly

28.

Sparingly praiſe thy Friend, leſt to thy Shame
Some one raſh Act his want of Worth proclaim.

29.

To learn whate'er thou knows not, think no Shame;
Knowledge juſt *Praiſe* deſerves, to want is *Blame*.

30.

From Love and Wine both Strife and Pleaſures ſpring;
Wiſely chuſe thou the *Sweet*, and ſhun the *Sting*.

31.

Of ſilent Men with Looks demure beware;
The *deepeſt* Streams the *ſmootheſt* Faces bear.

32.

When tempted at thy Fortune to repine,
Conſider thoſe whoſe Lot's ſtill worſe than thine.

33.

Know thy own Strength, and in due Limits keep;
The Shore is ſafe, but Danger's in the Deep.

34.

Againſt the Juſt try not the Force of Laws,
For God's th' Avenger of the righteous Cauſe.

35.

Let not the Loſs of Wealth thy Soul diſtreſs,
But chearful Thanks for every Good expreſs.

36.

Hard is the Loſs of what was held with Care,
Yet ſome for Friends we patiently ſhould bear.

37.

Don't on long Life preſumptuouſly depend,
Death, like thy Shade, does every where attend.

38. [peafe;

Think not Heav'n's Wrath with Blood of Calves t'ap-
The Plow's their Task, Incence will better pleafe.

39.

When hurt by Power, yield gently to the Blow;
For thofe that hurt, again may Favour fhow.

40.

For Sins on thy own Heart fharp Penance ftrain;
In healing Wounds Pain is the Cure of Pain.

41.

If an old Friend at length a Foe fhould prove,
Tho' he be chang'd remember former Love.

42.

By generous Returns thy felf endear,
Left thou th' hard Cenfure of ungrateful bear.

43.

Be not fufpicious, 'twill but give thee Pain;
Sufpicion's of all Joy the deadly Bane.

44.

Seize on Time's Forelock when it does prefent;
For when 'tis fled, in vain thou wilt repent.

45.

When thou a Servant buys, tho' term'd thy Slave,
He's Man, and Men a humane Treatment crave.

46.

Let not the Death of ill Men give thee Joy;
Who fpotlefs live may truly happy die.

47.

In Wedlock join'd, t'avoid a dangerous Snare,
Of Vifits from pretending Friends beware.

Tho'

48.

Tho' much thou knows, yet gain by Study more;
The Mind's ne'er burthen'd with th' enlightning Store.

49.

If couch'd in two flat Lines each Precept lies,
Yet brief and ſtrong the Senſe; let this ſuffice.
[*Sound pleaſes Fools, but Truth and Senſe the Wiſe.*]

F I N I S.

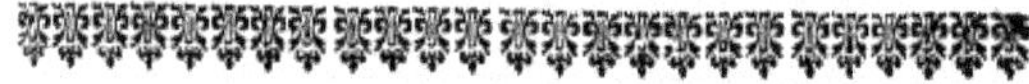

QUESTIONS AND DISCUSSION

Can you construe (big word just meaning 'translate') the 'literal' word-for-word-meaning of the text of the first and second distichs? (you may find it helpful to look at the two different translations given above: there are many others too – there's no one right way to translate a foreign text ...)

Which of the two translation do you prefer, and why?

Do you think that verse should be best translated into poetry or is prose sufficient? Why do you think this (a much-argued point among translators, your opinion is every bit as good as theirs).

If a friend gave you an English translation of one or more distichs could you turn them into Latin? Try ... (hard! But myself I find this quite the best way into appreciating the poet's art – and in English too: you could even try your hand at composing a few English 'distichs' too, and then enjoy criticising each others' efforts (constructively, of *course*!))

Contrary to traditional language teaching, grammatical rules are *not* the first thing to think about (as with English structures they emerge in/from the text rather than being something imposed onto it); but do you notice any recurrent 'grammatical' or 'syntactical' patterns in the distichs that draw you attention? [there are plenty] Does 'grammar' seem to be a constraint or an opportunity for Cato? (at this point – but better not before unless your teacher insists! - you might find it useful to look at some of the many Latin grammars and dictionaries available: go for a recent not an old-fashioned one, you can trace them on the web – or amazon)

During the first exercise (literal meanings), especially if you went on to look at several couplets, you may have been struck by the differences in word order as between Latin and English. Does the Latin order(s) have any advantages, especially for poetry, or is the Latin way of things just unnatural? (if you study other foreign languages you might also like to compare Latin with, say, German or Arabic in this respect)

Similarly for the metric and linguistic style

What other genres (styles/formats) of Latin literature have you come across (or found in some of the many encyclopaedias and reference works on the web)? Are they related in any way to English literary genres> or those in any other European languages you know about?

A lot of what Cato had to say is typical of the long tradition of 'Wisdom literature'. But, for nowadays, do you think anything of what Cato had to say is good advice? would you pass it on to your current girl/ boyfriend/ mother? (hm ...)

Do the *historical* and/or *religious* settings (plural rather than singular) throw any light on the *uses* people made of the distichs? (you can find loads on this and similar issues n the web if you're interested)

How many people altogether do you think learnt Latin from the distichs?(no I don't know either, but millions I should think – you are now one of them) There's no reason why you shouldn't go on to be every bit as good at Latin as Chaucer's carpenter or whoever – or better ....

Good luck - enjoy it!

CATO'S
DISTICHS

the longest-running Latin primer

in a new edition, with commentary, by
Ruth Finnegan

Callender Press 2013

ISBN 9781291546057

CONTENTS

Introduction

Cato's little distichs (or couplets) may be of little literary or philosophic importance in their own right,. But they have nonetheless had immeasurable influence in shaping the youth – and elders, and writers, and teachers- of countless generations, a school text in most countries of the then known worlds over centuries. As explained and illustrated in the accompanying essay, it stayed a best seller through centuries , effortlessly surviving the change from oral to manuscript to print, and is seemingly starting a revival today through the web.

This convenient edition is offered as an engaging text for learners of any age – how much more attractive than Caesar's marches through old-time

France or made-up texts about sailors seeing the table (or, if you're lucky) the girl. It offers a truly accessible experience of *real* Latin as it was lived for centuries, and can serve at the same time as an introduction to the great literary corpus of Rome and its cultural heritage. Through the ages.

Perhaps with this handy edition of text and translation it can again become a school text?[67]

CATO DISTICHS

Latin text and English verse translation

Preamble

Telluris si forte uelis cognoscere cultus, Uergilium legito; quodsi mage nosse laboras Herbarum uires, Macer haec tibi carmina dicit; Si Romana cupis et Punica noscere bella, Lucanum quaeres, qui Martis praelia dixit; Si quid amare libet uel discere amare legendo, Nasonem petito; sin autem cura tibi haec est, Ut sapien uiuas, audi quae discere possis, Per quae semotum uitiis deducitur aeuum: Ergo ades et quae sit sapientia disce legendo.]

If it chances that thou desirest to learn farming, read Virgil. But if thou strivest rather to know the potency of herbs, Macer tells thee of this in his poems. If thou wishest to know about the Roman and Punic wars, enquire of Lucan who tells of the combats of Mars. If it takes thy fancy to love something or to learn by reading how to love, have recourse to Naso. But if thy chief desire is to live wisely, hear what thou canst learn about those things through which an old age free from vice is produced. So come and learn by reading what wisdom is. [8]

Monostichs Deo *sntroductionupplica*. Parentes ama. Cognatos cole. Datum serua. Foro parce. Cum bonis ambula. Antequam uoceris, ne accesseris. Mundus esto. Saluta libenter. Maiori concede. Magistratum metue. Verecundiam serua. Rem tuam custodi. Diligentiam adhibe. Familiam cura. Mutuum da. Cui des, uideto. Conuiuare raro. Quod satis est, dormi. Coniugem ama. Iusiurandum serua. Uino tempera. Pugna pro patria. Nihil temere credideris. Meretricem fuge. Libros lege. Quae legeris, memento. Liberos erudi. Blandus esto. Irascere ob rem grauem. Neminem riseris. In

Pray to God. L
parents. Cheris
to thee. Guard
to thee. Shun t
place. Walk wi
Attack not unt
challenged. Be
freely. Yield to
older than tho
magistrate. Pre
sense of shame
thine own inter
diligence. Care
Return like for
well to whom t
presents. Indul
banquets. Slee
thy wife. Keep
moderate with
thy country. Be
imposed upon.
harlot. Read bo
Remember wh

iudicio adesto.

See to the instructic
children. Be kind.

Cato's Distichs through the centuries

The longevity of quotations collections such as those of Thomas of Ireland from the eleventh century and Erasmus' long-running *Adages*, amazing as these are, was dwarfed by the remarkable diffusion and continuity of a short work known as Cato's *Distichs*, a book happily going on its way alongside these other productions. Little read now, this collection of Latin moralistic epigrams became one of the best-known books in the Middle Ages and earlier, and remained in circulation for well over a millennium. For much of that time it was a best-seller in both manuscript and print[1]

It apparently originated in late antiquity, possibly the third century AD, when the name of Cato became attached to the collection. It was a series of short pieces of moral advice in Latin verse. These were not attributed to earlier writers but presented as precepts by Cato himself, or at any rate credited to him. Some probably went back to Greek originals and many carried reminiscences of Latin poets such as Horace,

Ovid, or Virgil, and at least one (2.3) was well-enough known to be quoted on an early gravestone:

Cease death to fear
none but a fool would choose
thro' fear of death the joys of life to lose.

'Cato's' collection came to be circulated as a store of memorable sayings in the same way as other compilations of quotation, had a huge circulation in many languages, and was extensively mined in later compilations of proverbs and moral maxims.

The book opened with a short prologue. As so often in the tradition of wisdom literature, the precepts were notionally addressed to the author's son:

When I noticed how very many go seriously wrong in their manner of living I concluded that I must apply a corrective to their belief and take counsel of the experience of mankind in order that they may live most gloriously and attain honour. Now I will teach thee, dearest son, in what way thou mayest fashion a rule for thy life. Therefore, so read my precepts that thou mayest understand them, for to read and not to understand is equivalent to not reading (Cato *Distichs*, Prologue, transl. Chase 1922).

Fifty-seven short one-line proverbial maxims followed, with pieces of practical and ethical advice like 'Yield to him who is older', 'Guard well your own interests', 'Keep your temper', 'Don't drink too much', 'Remember a good turn'.

The meat of the collection came in the following four books of (in all) 144 precepts in two-line classical Latin verse: the 'distichs' (couplets) of the title,l the Latin of antiquity reproduced here and still read by modern students and their teachers..

Slim as it was, the collection had a long life before it. It did not spring directly from the Christian tradition so, unlike Thomas of Ireland's huge compilation or Erasmus' learned collection, could not carry the authority of excerpts from revered writers. Nor did it have an alphabetical ordering or other device for easy searching. Yet it was a best seller for centuries, adopted and adapted by the Christian church and distributed across diverse countries and languages.

The central reason for this continuing popularity was its use in education. It served both as a key text for the learning of Latin and as a source of moral wisdom – albeit of a fairly practical and worldly kind - for instructing the young. It was read in Roman primary schools in later antiquity, studied in seventh-century monastery schools in Ireland, and in both the British Isles and the Continent was on school textbook lists in the eighth to eleventh-centuries. It was often bound together with other selected works in standard (if changing) combinations for school use, and from the fifteenth century taken up by printing presses across the western world.

Prized both as moral guide and Latin primer it helped to shape many lives over the centuries. More than just a schoolbook, it was read and valued by adults too, quoted both by scholars and in popular songs, and the couplets, often learned by heart during schooldays, left their trace through later years. Its verse style influenced later gnomic collections, and for centuries it was alluded to by writer after writer as a taken-for-granted text. It was referred to by the French poet Venantius Fortunatus in the sixth century and used by a long series of famous authors over the centuries, from Alcuin and Gerald of St Gall to the English Alfred the Great who, it was said, drew on it for his proverb collection. From the twelfth century on, as one author puts it, 'references to Cato ... are to be found literally everywhere' (Hazleton 1957: 159). The fourteenth-century *Piers Plowman* quoted plentifully from the *Distichs*, acknowledging the source. Chaucer was closely acquainted with the collection. His *Canterbury Tales* had many quotations – and parodies - from 'Catoun which that was so wys a man', and he could rely on his audience's understanding when he characterised a carpenter as without the most elementary of learning since 'He knew no Catoun, for his wit was rude'. Cato was mentioned in the prologue to *Don Quixote,* and both mediaeval and later German and Spanish writers quoted him extensively. By the fifteenth and sixteenth century parodies were circulating in the vernacular, as in the *Schoole of Slovenrie: or Cato Turn'd Wrong Side Outward* (1605). Its popularity was both demonstrated and enhanced by numerous commentaries and expositions in both mediaeval and more recent times, themselves built on for further exposition and circulation.

CATONIS
DISTICHA MORALIA EX CASTIGATIONE D. ERASMI ROTERODAMI

una cum annotationib9 & scholijs Richardi Tauerneri anglico idiomate conscriptis in usum Anglicæ iu-uentutis.

* * *

LONDINI.
Ex ædibus Richardi Tauerner.
Anno. M.D.XL.

Cum priuilegio ad imprimen-dum solum.

Title page of Richard Taverner's edition

Its massive diffusion also took place through innumerable translations – into, among other languages, French, German, Spanish, Danish, Dutch, Swedish, Italian, Polish, Hungarian, Irish, Anglo-Saxon, Anglo-Norman, Bohemian, Greek and Icelandic.

Four English editions of a version translated from the French were printed by William Caxton within seven years, the first in 1477; he dedicated it 'vnto the noble auncyent and renommed cyte [city] of London in Englond', directing it to the children of London merchants, as 'the best book to be taught to young children in school, and also to the people of every age it is full convenient if it be well understanded'. Erasmus quoted the book and brought out a version, itself widely translated and distributed in multiple editions, often bound together with other collections of wise sayings (Fig. 5.6 shows the title page of a London edition published in 1540). Another version, edited by Calvin's teacher Maturinus Corderius, was said to have gone through a hundred printings.

SEdechias was the first Philosophre by
through the wil and pleaser of oure lo
Sapience was understande and lawe
ued . Whiche Sedechias saide that eue
ture of good beleue ought to haue in hym sixtene v
¶ The first vertue is to drede and knowe god an
angellys ¶ The seconde vertue is to haue discrecion
twene the goode from the badde and to vse vertu an
vices ¶ The thirde vertue is to obeye the kynges or
that god hath ordeygned to regne vpon hym an
haue lordship and power vpon the people ¶ The f
vertue is to worship hys fadre & hys modre ¶ Th
vertue is to do Justely and truely to euery creatur
his possibilite ¶ The sixthe vertue is to distribute
mes to the pouer people. ¶ The seuenthe vertue is
and defende straungers and pilgrymes ¶ The

The first page of Caxton's print edition

In one form or another the book long continued in circulation. The Latin text was printed in 1577 as part of the Jesuits' educational programme in Mexico. It was used in English classrooms in the time of Milton and Oliver Cromwell, prescribed by sixteenth and seventeenth century statute for public schools like Eton and Harrow, and published with Erasmus' commentary in London in 1760 as *Cato's Distichs de moribus improved, in a more complete and useful method than any yet extant ... For the use of schools*. In both continental Europe and America its use in schools continued well into the eighteenth century in both Latin and vernacular. In 1735 Benjamin Franklin published a newly translated version in Philadelphia as *Cato's Moral Distichs Englished in Couplets* – the first Latin classic to be translated and printed in the British colonies of North America. He saw it as of good moral use for both adults and children – 'Very proper to be Put in the Hands of Young Persons' – and was confident that it would be in demand.

The Manuscript copy of this Translation of *Cato's Moral Distichs* happened into my Hands some time since, and being my self extremely pleased with it, I thought it might be no less acceptable to the Publick. ...In my Opinion it is no unfit or unprofitable Entertainment for those of riper Years. For certainly, such excellent Precepts of Morality, contain'd in such short and easily-remember'd

Sentences, may to Youth particularly be very serviceable in the Conduct of Life, since there can scarce happen any Affair of Importance to us, in which we may need Advice, but one or more of these Distichcs suited to the Occasion, will seasonably occur to the Memory, if the Book has been read and studied with a proper Care and Attention. ...

I confess, I have so great Confidence in the common Virtue and Good Sense of the People of this and the neighbouring Provinces, that I expect to sell a very good Impression (Franklin 1735: iii-iv).

Though Cato's text is no longer in print and is by now largely forgotten, it is gaining new life through circulation on the web and occasional surfacing in college courses. It even provided the 'quote for the day' (17th June) on a 2009 website, in its translation as:

Dread not the day that endeth all life's ills;
For fear of death all joy in living kills.

(helian.net/blog/2009/06/17/quote-for-today/quote-for-the-day-dionysius-cato-in-distichs/ 26 Nov. 2009).

These and other collections were constructed by their compilers from many, and varied, sources. The verbal clusters selected for record could be shorter or longer (sometimes just a single phrase or line); by unknown or by named (or misnamed) authors; and in a variety of familiar or unfamiliar languages. Depending on date or context they could be drawn from everyday or rhetorical speech, or – more often – from written sources: religious, literary, philosophical and much else, and presented under a variety of terms. Common at all periods, it seems, was some version of 'sayings' (Latin *dicta*) but with changing targets and connotations over the centuries. The 'authorities' of early collections, whether Christian or from the ancient classical world, gradually gave way or were combined with less normative terms like 'maxims', 'commonplaces' (with its changing meanings), 'proverbs', 'adages', the overarching term 'quotations' or, most recently, 'catchphrases', 'songs' and 'slogans'.

The selections were also of course bound into that same question as in the previous chapter: of whose voices and what kind of excerpts counted as suitable for highlighting, repeating and – in the present context – storing for further reference. Attitudes to the collecting of others' words have in part paralleled the changing uses of quote marks, as they gradually moved from focusing primarily on classical, literary or authoritative Christian sources to sayings from the near-present, from the 'common man, and from spoken not just written language. By the nineteenth century newspapers as well as literary and biblical sources were being drawn on and, though the idea of 'best authors' still prevailed, nineteenth- and, especially, twentieth-century quotation collections laid particular stress on 'familiar', 'popular', or 'in most frequent' or 'common' use. Not that that avoided the issue of *whose* definition of 'familiar' counted and who controlled the selection. In the sixteenth century Erasmus had presented his adages as 'frequently on people's lips' while looking to the ancient classic writers for his selection and despising the verbalisation of the common people, while the 'literary reader' of the 1941 *Oxford Dictionary of Quotations* might scarcely fit the common expectations of today. But the trawl has now certainly spread to include wording from film, broadcast and 'non-traditional' media, extending beyond the traditional literary canon of just one country. Recent collections boast of being up to the minute and pride themselves on including 'new', 'modern' and 'topical' quotes.

But at same time another striking feature of recent collections – even now - is a continuing interest in spanning the ages. Contemporary blurbs swim with phrases like 'from Cleopatra to J. K. Rowling, and the battle of Marathon to the Hutton inquiry', 'from the ancients of East and West to the global village of the twenty-first century', 'from Cicero to the Simpsons'. The sources come from past as well as present and, as in earlier collections, there remains a focus on the wealth and wisdom of past times. Even now allusions to the classical world carry surprising resonance and many collections still contain quotations from Latin or Greek and the high-art literary canon from earlier centuries, and refer in their blurbs to the authors of antiquity. Looking to the past not just the present almost seems a requirement for what it is to be a collection of quotations.

This is reinforced by the remarkable longevity of many key collections and their impact both across vast geographical areas and on successive generations. In their presence and travels they transmit, and embody, voices from beyond the present.

The Dictes and Sayings of the Philosophers published by William Caxton in 1477 is an example of one such compilations. That it should be the first book to be printed with a date in England evidences the interest in such collections while its curious history illustrates well both their long-lived potential and the complex and far-reaching pathways they sometimes followed. The Arabic original of this work had been compiled in Cairo near the start of the second millennium by the Syrian Mubashshir ibn Fatik as *Muhtar-al-Hikam* ('Wise sayings'). It appeared in 1053 with its hundreds of quotations from Jewish, Arabic and Greek sources. Two centuries later it was circulating in Spanish translation as *Bocados de Oro* ('Gold sayings'). It was soon translated further into Latin, cut down to just the philosophers' sayings, and circulated widely in Europe under such titles as *Liber philosophorum moralium* or *Placita philosophorum.* In the late fourteenth century it appeared in French as *Les dits des philosophes*. Both Latin and French versions became popular in England and at least four English translations were in circulation in the mid to late fifteenth century, with many changes and errors accumulated over the centuries. Caxton's 1477 publication was a translation from the French version into English by the king's brother-in-law Earl

Rivers who paid Caxton to print and edit it (on this (arguably controversial) work see Raybould 2006, Jayne 1995: 37ff).)

Except in its remarkable long life, extended here, Cato's *Distichs* were far from unparallelled, a notable feature of the long-standing, and surely still valued, culture of Europe, and beyond Europe now offered once more to contemporary readers.

A collection of such longevity surely tells us something about the European devotion to written repositories of verbal sayings. Over the centuries there have indeed been many great literary works and collections but there can have been few which directly touched so many lives over a millennium or more as this modest compilation of maxims. A long tradition unquestionably underpins the quotation collections of today.

Note: I have drawn especially on Chase 1922 and Duff and Duff 1935, also on Boas 1952, Hazelton 1957, 1960, Marchand 2006/2009,

Taylor 1992, 1999, 2004; see also references below. The traditional attribution to the earlier Roman statesman Marcius Portius Cato and the added name of Dionysius are rejected by modern scholars.

References

Boas, Marcus (ed.) (1952) *Disticha Catonis*, Amsterdam: North-Holland Publishing.

Chase, Wayland Johnson (1922) *The Distichs of Cato. A Famous Medieval Textbook*, Madison: University of Wisconsin Studies in the Social Sciences and History 7.

Duff, John Wight and Duff, Arnold Mackay (eds) (1935) *Minor Latin Poets*, London: Heinemann.

Finnegan, Ruth (2011) *Why Do We Quote? The Culture and History of Quotation*, Cambridge: Open Book, chapter 5 (also www.openbookpublishers.com/product.php/75/18/-why-do-we-quote--the-culture-and-history-of-quotation/)

Hazelton, Richard (1957) 'The Christianization of "Cato": the *Disticha Catonis* in the light of late mediaeval commentaries', *Mediaeval Studies* 19: 164-7.

Marchand, James and Irvine, Martin (eds and transl.) (2006/2009) *Cato's Distichs* http://ccat.sas.upenn.edu/jod/texts/monostich.html (July 2006), possibly replaced by www9.georgetown.edu/faculty/jod/texts/cato.html (15 Nov. 2009).

Taylor, Barry (1999) 'Michael Verinus and the *Distichs* of Cato in Spain: a comparative study in reception', in Taylor, Barry and Coroleu, Alejandro (eds) *Latin and Vernacular in Renaissance Spain*, Manchester: Manchester Spanish and Portuguese Studies.

Taylor, Barry (ed. and transl.) (2004) *Alonso de Cartagena(?) Cathoniana Confectio*, Bristol: HiPLAM. 42

Here foloweth The lyf of Saynt Jherome And first of his name

Jherome is sayd of Jherar that is holy / And of nemus / that is to saye a woode / And soo Jherome

PHIL

Printed and Sold by

sion, will seasonably occur to the Memory, if the Book been read and studied with a proper Care and Attention.

When I obtained Leave to make this Publication, I p cured also the following Account of the Author and Work: for I thought something of the kind necessary to prefix'd to it.

*In most Places that I am acquainted with, so grea the present Corruption of Manners, that a Printer s find much more Profit in such Things as flatter and enc rage Vice, than in such as tend to promote its contra It would be thought a Piece of Hypocrisy and pharisa Ostentation in me, if I should say, that I print these D*tichs *more with a View to the Good of others than my o private Advantage: And indeed I cannot say it; for I c fess, I have so great Confidence in the common Virtue Good Sense of the People of this and the neighbouring P vinces, that I expect to sell a very good Impression.*

Som

The PRINTER to the READER.

THE *Manuſcript Copy of this Tranſlation of* Cato's Moral Diſtichs, *happened into my Hands ſome Time ſince, and being my ſelf extreamly pleaſed with it, I thought it might be no leſs acceptable to the Publick; and therefore determined to print it as ſoon as I ſhould have convenient Leiſure and Opportunity. It was done by a Gentleman amongſt us (whoſe Name or Character I am ſtrictly forbid to mention, tho' it might give ſome Advantage to my Edition) for the Uſe of his own Children; But in my Opinion, it is no unfit or unprofitable Entertainment for thoſe of riper Years. For certainly, ſuch excellent Precepts of Morality, contain'd in ſuch ſhort and eaſily-remember'd Sentences, may to Youth particularly be very ſerviceable in the Conduct of Life, ſince there can ſcarce happen any Affair of Importance to us, in which we may need Advice, but one or more of theſe Diſtichs ſuited to the Occa-*

 ſion,

Some ACCOUNT of the following Piece, and Conjectures concerning its AUTHOR.

THO' the Original of these Moral Distichs, by being put into the Hands of Boys of the lower Forms at the Latin School, have been frequently considered as an Entertainment suitable only to such childish Years; yet great and able Judges have conceived a much more honourable Esteem of them. They have been commented on by divers Authors, but particularly by *Erasmus*: They were translated into Greek by *Maximus Planudes*, a native of *Greece*, and one of the most learned of his Age. But the great *Joseph Scaliger*, dissatisfyed with that Performance, gave another most elegant Version of them into the same Language, which has been divers times printed. And tho' a Critic in that Tongue, on viewing the Version, would not easily be induced to believe it could be better'd, yet it has been twice since attempted by two other several Hands, mentioned by *Fabricius*. So that at least four Greek Translations of them have appeared. Into the European Languages, as French, Italian, Dutch, there have been many Translations, and into each of them by several Hands. They have also been divers Times render'd into our own; but the Author of this never saw any of them, that by *Charles Hoole*, made in plain and low Language for the Use of School-boys, only excepted; and therefore he knows not but they may have been much better done before: But as he intended them (as they are here finished) solely for the Use of his own Children, with some of their Acquaintance, and never for publick View, he is no way solicitous what others may have perform'd, provided these as they are, will answer the End they were intended for. Those who find Fault with them may try to do better on any Score of them together, and then they will be more capable of judging, whether it is a very easy Task throughout the

whole

CATO's

MORAL DISTICHS.

1.

IF God be Spirit, as old Texts aſſure,
Him chief o'er all with pureſt mind adore.

2.

Be ſtill induſtrious, too much Sleep refrain;
For Vice from Sloth does conſtant Succours gain.

3.

Think the firſt Virtue's well to rule the Tongue;
He's godlike wiſe, who ne'er employs it wrong.

4.

Conſiſtent always with thy ſelf be found;
Who thwarts himſelf, would thwart all Mankind round.

5.

If o'er Mens Lives and Deeds thou caſt an Eye,
While all ſpy Faults, free from them none thou'lt ſpy.

The

6.

The Charms of hurtful Joys, tho' ſweet, refuſe:
'Tis ſometimes Gain ev'n Wealth itſelf to loſe.

7.

Or grave or gay appear, to ſuit the Time:
The Wiſe may Manners change without a Crime.

8.

Let not your Wife's weak Humours Anger move
Againſt a Servant you've juſt Cauſe to love.

9.

When thou reproves a Friend, tho' ſcarce he'll bear
Tho' much he frown, continue ſtill thy Care.

10.

Wage not with Men of Words, a noiſy War;
Words *all* have got, *Few* Wiſdom to their Share.

11.

So love thy Friends, and ſo thy Favours deal,
As that thy ſelf their Want may never feel.

12.

Spread not Reports, leſt they be thought thy own:
From Tatling Miſchief ſprings, from Silence none.

13.

Let not *another's* Promiſe *thine* engage
To plight thy Faith; 'tis now a faithleſs Age.

14.

When others praiſe thee, judge thy ſelf alone;
Better thou'rt to thy ſelf than others known.

15.

A Friend's good Offices aloud proclaim;
But thy good Deeds to others never name.

16.

While in Old-age you others Conduct tell,
Think whether in your Youth your own was well.

17

What Men in private whisper, never mind;
The Guilty always think themselves design'd.

18.

While Fortune's smiling, bear a watchful Eye
On her Reverse, her Favours swiftly fly.

19.

Since on so frail a Tenure Life is held,
Thy Hopes on Death's Reversions never build.

20.

The poor Man's Present from his scanty Store
With Thanks receive, as if its Worth were more.

21.

Since Nature form'd thee naked in the Womb,
Grudge not at Want; it does thy State become.

22.

Fear not the End of Life, it ends thy Care;
He present Life destroys, who Death does fear.

23.

When to thy Merit, Friends ungrateful prove,
Accuse not Heaven, but with more Judgment love.

24.

Spare but to spend, and Spending spare so well,
As neither *now* nor *after* want to feel.

25.

Promise not twice what may at once be done,
Lest thou be bounteous deem'd in *Words* alone.

26.

Him, who is kind in *Words*, but false in *Heart*,
In his own Coin repay, with Art for Art.
[*Yet with unblemish'd Honour act thy Part.*]

27.

No Stress on smooth-tongu'd Mens Professions lay
Sweet plays the Fowler's Pipe to gain his Prey.

28.

If thou hast Children, but no Wealth to give,
Then teach them Arts, that they may learn to liv

29.

Mean things as Great, great things as *Mean* esteem
So neither *prodigal* nor *near* thou'lt seem.

30.

Act not thy self what thou art wont to blame;
When Teachers slip themselves, 'tis double Shame

31.

Crave what is Just and Honest, nought beside;
'Tis vain to ask what may be well deny'd.

32.

Th' unknown to what thou knows do not prefer;
For Judgment governs *here*, Chance only *there*.

33.

Since Life's frail Course through certain Danger
Each new-come Day as a new Purchase prize.

34.

Tho' in the right, yield sometimes to a Friend;
Friendship by kind Complaisance is maintain'd.

35.

In quest of greater Matters, spare not small;
'Tis Profit that in Love unites us all.

W

36.

With Intimates no trifling Quarrels move;
Wrath *Hate* begets, Concord increafes Love.

37.

When Servants Failings thy Refentments warm,
Thy Anger check, left thou their Perfons harm.

38.

Your Friends o'ercome not always when you can;
For Patience often fpeaks the greater Man.

39.

What thou haft gain'd with Toil, preferve with Care:
Heavy's the Task paft Loffes to repair.

40.

In Plenty let thy Friends thy Bounty fhare;
Yet make they felf thy moft peculiar Care.

BOOK II.

YOU who in Husbandry would Skill attain,
May *Virgil* read; or if you'd Knowledge gain
In healing Plants, thefe you'll in *Macer* find,
With Cures prefcrib'd for Ails of every kind.
If Civil Wars and *Rome*'s fad Broils you'd know,
Lucan thofe dire Exploits of *Mars* will fhow.
Or if by Rules you'd guide Love's gentler Flame,
Ovid confult: But if your nobler Aim
To fteer your Life by Wifdom's Laws afpire,
Read here, and learn the Prudence you defire.

1. Even

1.

Even to Strangers thy good Deeds extend;
'Tis better than a Crown to gain a Friend.

2.

Search not God's Secrets, nor his Works on high;
Mind what concerns thee as thou'rt born to die.

3.

Avoid the Fear of *Death*, it idle shews
For fear of losing *Life*, its *Joys* to lose.

4.

Of Doubts contend not in an angry mind:
Wrath clouds the Soul, and does the Judgment blin[d]

5.

Genteely spend as Circumstances crave:
'Tis sometimes *Loss* penuriously to *save*.

6.

Avoid Excess, pursue the Golden Mean;
'Tis safest Sailing in the gentle Stream.

7.

What gives thee Shame, reveal not unto more,
Lest *Many* blame what but *One* blam'd before.

8.

Think not th'Unrighteous in their Crimes succeed;
Time that conceals reveals an impious Deed.

9.

No feebler Creature's Want of Strength despise;
For Nature Want of Strength by Skill supplies.

10.

When over-match'd, in time resolve to yield;
Thus oft the Victor's by the Vanquish'd foil'd.

Sh[e]

11.

Shun with thy Friends contentious Words to uſe;
For Diſcord oft from trifling Words enſues.

12.

All Search of Fate by Divination fly:
God without thee thy Lot decrees on high.

13.

Create not Envy by a ſumptuous Dreſs;
For tho' it hurts not, 't may affect thy Peace.

14.

Be not diſmay'd when Judges do thee Wrong;
The Cauſe that's gain'd unjuſtly, thrives not long.

15.

In Quarrels paſt name not what was unkind:
To think on't argues an ungenerous Mind.

16.

Nor praiſe nor blame thy ſelf, for only Fools
Thus court Vain-glory by prepoſterous Rules.

17.

Manage with Care thy Wealth, Expence reſtrain;
Th' Eſtate's ſoon loſt that took long time to gain.

18.

A Fool, when there's Occaſion for't, appear;
'Tis ſometimes *Wiſdom*, *Folly*'s Mask to wear.

19.

With equal care avoid a Miſer's Name
And *Prodigal*'s; they both will wound thy Fame.

20.

Believe not all, ſome kind of People tell;
They talk not always true, who talk a deal.

21.

Forgive not what thou doſt provok'd by Wine;
'Tis not the Liquor's fault; to drink was *Thine.*

22.

Thy Counſels to a truſty Friend declare;
Thy Health commit to wiſe Phyſicians Care.

23.

At worthleſs Mens Advancement never grieve:
Who higheſt mount, the heavieſt Fall receive.

24.

Still for the Worſt to come, thy Mind prepare;
So with more Eaſe thou Ills foreſeen wilt bear.

25.

In adverſe Times let not thy Courage fail:
Still hope, 'gainſt Hope ev'n Death can ſcarce prevail.

26.

Slip not the Seaſon when it ſuits thy Mind;
Time wears his Lock *before*, is bald *behind.*

27.

View well what's paſt, and what may next enſue,
And Janus-like at once both Seaſons view.

28.

Thy Health to guard, Pleaſures ſometimes refrain;
To Pleaſure ſomewhat give, but Health's the Main.

29.

Slight not the general Vogue while thou'rt but one,
Leſt while thou ſlights the moſt thou pleaſes none.

30.

Manage thy Health 'bove all with prudent Care,
Nor for thy Follies blame th' unwholeſome Air.

Regard

31.
Regard not Dreams, the Mind will ſtill purſue
In *Sleep*, what *waking* it had moſt in View.

BOOK III.

WHOE'ER will on theſe Lines ſome Thoughts beſtow,
Which wholeſome Rules for Life's ſure Conduct ſhow,
Will reap th' Advantage: Thoſe who them deſpiſe
Will prove not *mine*, but *their own* Enemies.

1.
No Pains t' adorn thy Mind with Knowledge ſpare;
Without it Life does Death's dull Image bear.

2.
For Loſs of Pelf 'gainſt Fortune don't exclaim;
Virtue not Wealth gives Happineſs and Fame.

3.
Scandal, while thou uprightly acts, deride:
'Tis not in human Power Mens Tongues to guide.

4.
When as an Evidence thou muſt appear,
Favour thy Friend, but keep thy Conſcience clear.

5.
Againſt ſoft ſoothing Speeches guard thy Heart;
Truth Plainneſs chooſes, *Fraud* diſſembling Art.

6.
To Sloth, Life's great Conſumption, give not way;
Sloth in the *Mind* does on the Body prey.

By

17.

When Laws oppreſs, Aid from the Judge deſire;
For Laws ſome Mitigation oft require.

18.

What thou from Juſtice ſuffers, calmly bear,
And on thy Guilt thy ſelf be moſt ſevere.

19.

Read much, and much of that when read reject;
For Poets Wonders more than Truth affect.

20.

At Feaſts in Talk be modeſt, leſt thou gain
A Trifler's Name while ſtudying t' entertain.

21.

Regard not Woman's Paſſions, nor her Smiles:
With *Paſſion* ſhe enſnares, with *Tears* beguiles.

22.

Enjoy thy Goods, but let no Waſte be made:
Who waſtes his own, will others Right invade.

23.

Firmly reſolv'd, Death's Summons ſcorn to fear,
Which if not lovely, ends at leaſt all Care.

24.

If thy Wiſe's virtuous, bear her Tongue, for ſure
Thou may'ſt for her good Deeds ſome Words endure.

25.

Equal Affection for both Parents bear;
Nor ſlight the one the other to revere.

BOOK IV.

YOU who a Life ſecure from Ills would lead,
And Virtue's Paths by Vice untainted tread,
Firmly impreſs theſe Precepts on your Mind,
Here by your ſelf you'll ſafe Direction find.

1.

Riches contemn if thou true Bliſs would find;
Who honour theſe, are Beggars in their Mind.

2.

If by wiſe Nature's Rules thou bounds Deſires,
Thou'lt eaſy live; 'tis little ſhe requires.

3.

For Ills that from thy own Imprudence came,
Thy own weak Folly not thy Fortune blame.

4.

The Uſe of Money not the Metal prize;
Souls truly great will ever that deſpiſe.

5.

To keep thy Body ſound, ſpare not thy Wealth:
Riches are taſteleſs when not bleſt with Health.

6.

If when at School the Maſter's Rod thou bore,
Bear with a Parent's Anger much the more.

7.

In Things of real Uſe thy Time employ;
Vain Projects Time and Money both deſtroy.

8.

Sell not thy Favours through unkind Delays,
But Friends, the nobleſt Purchaſe, with them raiſe.

9.

When thou ſuſpects a Miſchief, ſtrait enquire;
Neglected Sparks oft raiſe deſtructive Fire.

10.

When *Venus* through thy Blood enflames Deſire,
Retrench thy Food; high Feeding fans the Fire.

11.

Devouring Beaſts Man juſtly dreads, yet know
That Man to Man is the moſt *dreadful Foe.*

12.

If thou excells in Strength, direct it well;
So may thou in true Valour too excel.

13.

In Straits a well-prov'd Friend's Aſſiſtance crave:
In Straits no Doctor like a Friend can ſave.

14.

Why for thy Guilt ſhould guiltleſs Victims bleed;
By others Death thou cann't from Death be freed.

15.

When ſome true Boſom-Friend thou ſeeks to chooſe,
Let Wiſdom and not Wealth direct thy Views.

16.

Vile Avarice deteſt, enjoy thy Store:
The Miſer midſt his Heaps of Wealth is poor.

17.

If thou a Fame unblemiſh'd would'ſt maintain,
Th' alluring Charms of Vice with Care refrain.

18.

In Youth mock not old Age; Youth swiftly spends
And double Childhood human Life attends.

19.

Still learn some useful Thing, for small's the Cost,
Yet that may hold when all Things else are lost.

20.

In Silence ponder well what others say:
Words oft the Speaker's inward Soul betray.

21.

When thou hast gain'd a Science, practice still;
Practice in every Art improves the Skill.

22.

With future Ills thy Soul ne'er terrify:
Who Life despises needs not fear to die.

23.

Learn of the Learn'd, and others teach again,
That useful Knowledge thro' the World may reign

24.

Drink not beyond thy Strength; for from Excess
Disorders spring that the whole Frame distress.

25.

What you've approv'd in publick, don't again
Condemn through Lightness; 'twill your Credit sta

26.

In *prosperous* Times don't on their Stay presume:
In *adverse*, hope for better still to come,

27.

Cease not to learn, Wisdom's by Care attain'd,
And Prudence from a long Experience gain'd.

Sparing

28.

Sparingly praiſe thy Friend, leſt to thy Shame
Some one raſh Act his want of Worth proclaim.

29.

To learn whate'er thou knows not, think no Shame;
Knowledge juſt *Praiſe* deſerves, to want is *Blame.*

30.

From Love and Wine both Strife and Pleaſures ſpring;
Wiſely chuſe thou the *Sweet*, and ſhun the *Sting.*

31.

Of ſilent Men with Looks demure beware;
The *deepeſt* Streams the *ſmootheſt* Faces bear.

32.

When tempted at thy Fortune to repine,
Conſider thoſe whoſe Lot's ſtill worſe than thine.

33.

Know thy own Strength, and in due Limits keep;
The Shore is ſafe, but Danger's in the Deep.

34.

Againſt the Juſt try not the Force of Laws,
For God's th' Avenger of the righteous Cauſe.

35.

Let not the Loſs of Wealth thy Soul diſtreſs,
But chearful Thanks for every Good expreſs.

36.

Hard is the Loſs of what was held with Care,
Yet ſome for Friends we patiently ſhould bear.

37.

Don't on long Life preſumptuouſly depend,
Death, like thy Shade, does every where attend.

38. [peas

Think not Heav'n's Wrath with Blood of Calves t'a
The Plow's their Task, Incence will better please.

39.

When hurt by Power, yield gently to the Blow;
For those that hurt, again may Favour show.

40.

For Sins on thy own Heart sharp Penance strain;
In healing Wounds Pain is the Cure of Pain.

41.

If an old Friend at length a Foe should prove,
Tho' he be chang'd remember former Love.

42.

By generous Returns thy self endear,
Lest thou th' hard Censure of ungrateful bear.

43.

Be not suspicious, 'twill but give thee Pain;
Suspicion's of all Joy the deadly Bane.

44.

Seize on Time's Forelock when it does present;
For when 'tis fled, in vain thou wilt repent.

45.

When thou a Servant buys, tho' term'd thy Slave,
He's Man, and Men a humane Treatment crave.

46.

Let not the Death of ill Men give thee Joy;
Who spotless live may truly happy die.

47.

In Wedlock join'd, t' avoid a dangerous Snare,
Of Visits from pretending Friends beware.

48.

Tho' much thou knows, yet gain by Study more;
The Mind's ne'er burthen'd with th' enlightning Store.

49.

If couch'd in two flat Lines each Precept lies,
Yet brief and ſtrong the Senſe; let this ſuffice.
[*Sound pleaſes Fools, but Truth and Senſe the Wiſe.*]

F I N I S.

QUESTIONS AND DISCUSSION

Can you construe (big word just meaning 'translate') the 'literal' word-for-word-meaning of the text of the first and second distichs? (you may find it helpful to look at the two different translations given above: there are many others too – there's no one right way to translate a foreign text ...)

Which of the two translation do you prefer, and why?

Do you think that verse should be best translated into poetry or is prose sufficient? Why do you think this (a much-argued point among translators, your opinion is every bit as good as theirs).

If a friend gave you an English translation of one or more distichs could you turn them into Latin? Try ... (hard! But myself I find this quite the best way into appreciating the poet's art – and in English too: you could even try your hand at composing a few English 'distichs' too, and then enjoy criticising each others' efforts (constructively, of *course*!))

Contrary to traditional language teaching, grammatical rules are *not* the first thing to think about (as with English structures they emerge in/from the text rather than being something imposed onto it); but do you notice any recurrent 'grammatical' or 'syntactical' patterns in the distichs that draw you attention? [there are plenty] Does 'grammar' seem to be a constraint or an opportunity for Cato? (at this point – but better not before unless your teacher insists! - you might find it useful to look at some of the many Latin grammars and dictionaries available: go for a recent not an old-fashioned one, you can trace them on the web – or amazon)

During the first exercise (literal meanings), especially if you went on to look at several couplets, you may have been struck by the 70 differences in word order as between Latin and English. Does the Latin order(s) have any advantages, especially for poetry, or is the Latin way of things just unnatural? (if you study other foreign languages you might also like to compare Latin with, say, German or Arabic in this respect)

Similarly for the metric and linguistic style

What other genres (styles/formats) of Latin literature have you come across (or found in some of the many encyclopaedias and reference works on the web)? Are they related in any way to English literary genres> or those in any other European languages you know about?

A lot of what Cato had to say is typical of the long tradition of 'Wisdom literature'. But, for nowadays, do you think anything of what Cato had to say is good advice? would you pass it on to your current girl/ boyfriend/ mother? (hm ...)

Do the *historical* and/or *religious* settings (plural rather than singular) throw any light on the *uses* people made of the distichs? (you can find loads on this and similar issues n the web if you're interested)

How many people altogether do you think learnt Latin from the distichs?(no I don't know either, but millions I should think – you are now one of them) There's no reason why you shouldn't go on to be every bit as good at Latin as Chaucer's carpenter or whoever – or better ....

Good luck - enjoy it!

www.ingramcontent.com/pod-product-compliance
Ingram Content Group UK Ltd.
Pitfield, Milton Keynes, MK11 3LW, UK
UKHW020238250726
13967UKWH00001B/436

9 781291 546057